Contents

COAST & CLIFFTOP BIRDS

A
Birdwatching
Logbook

Birdwatching Tips

The aim of this series is to encourage you to look out for the birds around you, and record when and where you see them.

It is important to get to know how a bird moves, flies, and sings as well as identifying the shape, so the illustrations are there to show you important features to look out for, and the accompanying text tells you how the bird behaves.

Becoming familiar with common birds allows you to spot rarer sightings, so this book is to help you practise your birdcraft and enable you to become acquainted with the birds in your area and beyond.

Fratercula arctica

Body length: *28-34cm*

Where to spot:

Out at sea, steep cliffs,

grassy areas nearby

Summer visitor

PUFFIN

Everybody knows these iconic seabirds, with their bright, parrot-like bill and clown eyes. They nest in burrows on the grassy slopes above cliffs, and feed on sand eels which they gather up in their striped bills.

They have a fast-flapping flight and spend the winter out on the ocean, bobbing around sitting high on the water. The bill loses some of its drama in winter as the colours are there to impress their mate, with whom they form an enduring partnership over their 30 year lifespan.

The call is a cross between a groan and a croak.

Date	Notes

RINGED PLOVER

Charadrius hiaticula

Body length: *16-18cm*

Where to spot:

Estuaries, mudflats,

reservoirs, gravel pits

Resident

The black eye mask, white breast and sandy-brown back of a ringed plover means this thrush-sized bird is easily recognisable. They feed on invertebrates so are likely to be seen in a variety of environments, both marine and freshwater, as they search for food.

Although we have a resident population, the numbers fluctuate as the birds move from summer breeding sites to winter feeding sites, and migrants join and then move on. This is the case for many of 'our' birds.

A gentle, upward-lilting "doo-eep" is the call.

Date	Notes

Haematopus ostralegus

Body length: *39-44cm*

Where to spot:

Tidal flats, shoreline, fields

nearby

Resident

OYSTERCATCHER

Oystercatchers are so evocative of wetlands and estuaries, and their large size, pied plumage coupled with pink legs and bright orange bill render them unmistakeable.

Despite their name, they mainly feed on cockles and mussels, as well as other invertebrates buried in the sand and stones. That long robust bill can be used either as a chisel to prise open the shells, or as a blunt instrument to hammer their way in. Like puffins, they are long-lived birds and can survive well in to their 30s.

The call is a high-pitched, repetitive "keep keep keeeep".

Date	Notes

RAVEN

Corvus corax

Body length: *54-67cm*

Where to spot:

Cliff ledges, hilly upland

areas

Resident

Our largest crow - and indeed passerine (perching bird). Ravens breed on cliffs, and roam scarp slopes and upland and hilly areas nearby looking for food which is often carrion, but they do take small birds and mammals as well as insects and other invertebrates.

They really are large, and have a definite wedge-shaped tail and a rounded wing profile with primary feathers splayed when soaring on a thermal.

The call is a classic "korrr-korrr" but a deeper, richer sound compared to other corvids.

Date	Notes

Oenanthe oenanthe

Body length: *14-16cm*

Where to spot:

Coastal grassland, shingle

banks, seaside towns

Summer visitor

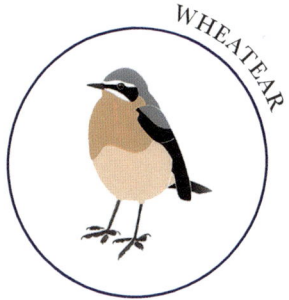

WHEATEAR

The upright stance of this pretty bird indicates it is a member of the thrush family. Wheatears visit our country during the summer having wintered in Africa, and so are often seen on passage around coasts as they make their way to breeding grounds. In flight, the white tail with black T-bar is very distinctive as they flit between their insect hunting grounds.

Females are more creamy and rufous in their colouring, and lack the striking black eye mask of the males.

A wheatear's song is a short, buzzy ditty.

Date	Notes

PEREGRINE FALCON

Falco peregrinus

Body length: *38-51cm*

Where to spot:

Cliffs and steep slopes,

marshland, floodplains

Resident

Muscular and stocky, the peregrine falcon is rightly renowned for its prowess in the skies. It nests on cliffs and hunts small and medium birds from its lofty vantage point, catching them in mid-air following a steep nosedive at great speed.

The plumage is a steely-grey back with a broad black moustache and barred chest. Juveniles are brown but otherwise marked the same.

The eerie and piercing cry is a commanding sound, made more noticeable as the surrounding birds will fall silent.

Date	Notes

Somateria mollissima

Body length: *60-70cm*

Where to spot:

Open sea, coastal waters,

archipelagos

Resident

EIDER

Male eiders are large and handsome seaducks, with olive green legs, nape, and wedge-shaped bill. They breed in coastal areas and feed in marine environs, diving some metres to forage for molluscs and crustaceans.

Females are stripy brown which helps camouflage them as they sit on feathered nests, from where we get the word 'eiderdown'.

The rather nasal and quizzical "noo-ooo" is used frequently by the males during courtship, whereas the female has more of a throbby chuckle.

Date	Notes

Larus argentatus

Body length: *54-60cm*

Where to spot:

All along coastal towns

and harbours

Resident

The archetypal 'seagull' with a predilection for chips. They are found in many places but love them or hate them, they are part and parcel of our seaside experience.

These large gulls have grey backs, pink legs, and that little red spot on a yellow bill, although they take 4 years to reach this classic plumage being much more brown and mottled as a youngster.

Their call is very familiar: loud, frequent and varying from a robust "kyew" as well as a more rapid quickfire "ag-ag-ag" when alarmed.

Date	Notes

Larus ridibundus

Body length: *35-39cm*

Where to spot:

Coastal towns, marshes,

ponds, reedbeds, fields

Resident

BLACK-HEADED GULL

Often found in towns and on farms as well as by the sea, these dainty gulls are confident and often gather in large numbers to roost and feed.

The chocolate-brown head is only present in the summer plumage of adults, and 1st-winter birds are delightfully checkered with ochre, black, white and grey feathers. In winter, the dark hood reduces to a dot behind the eye for all age groups.

The call is noisy and has a downward intonation making it sound rather scolding and full of disapproval.

Date	Notes

Use this page as a quick ticklist

Date
completed:

SNOW BUNTING

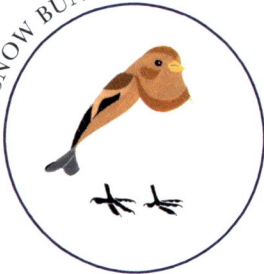

Plectrophenax nivalis

Body length: *15-18cm*

Where to spot:

Shoreline, coastal pasture,

rough ground nearby

Winter visitor

Buntings are like stripy finches, and these breed in high latitudes where they moult their patterned plumage, turning white with a dark back and wings.

They arrive in autumn looking for food which is mostly the seeds of grasses. As such, their numbers and location vary, but they can gather in large dense flocks along the shores, looking like a flurry of snow as they move.

As with all buntings, they have a tuneful repertoire and use a variety of buzzes and whistles to communicate within the flock.

Date	Notes

Phalacrocorax aristotelis

Body length: *68-78cm*

Where to spot:

Coastal cliffs and along

shoreline

Resident

SHAG

These colonial birds are smaller than cormorants, although they have a very similar shape and are easily confused when seen standing on a pier or harbour wall. They have no white feathers, however, instead sporting an attractive glossy green plumage during the breeding season and a topknot crest on their forehead. They are birds of the coast and are rarely seen inland.

When feeding, they often leap clear of the water before diving for fish.

They rarely speak when away from the colony.

Date	Notes

SHELDUCK

Tadorna tadorna

Body length: *55-65cm*

Where to spot:

Open shorelines, grassy areas, coastal pasture

Resident

These boldly-patterned ducks are quite goose-like in shape, and flocks of them will congregate along estuaries, coastlines, reservoirs and other large bodies of water as they look for snails and shellfish. Sheldrakes have a large knob at the top of the bill which the female lacks.

They nest in burrows and waddle their black and white stripy ducklings down to the shore, often leaving them clustered in a creche looking like a collection of mint humbugs.

Their call is a hissy, high-pitched quack.

Date	Notes

Riparia riparia

Body length: *12-13cm*

Where to spot:

Sandy banks and steep

earthy cliffs

Summer visitor

SAND MARTIN

These small martins return from their West African summer residence to make the most of our insects to raise their young, roosting in large numbers in reedbeds. They return to favoured sites to nest communally in steep earth banks where they dig a burrow over a metre in length to protect the eggs and hatchlings.

They have a brown back and a creamy-white underside with a band across the throat.

A chattering dry rasp is heard when they are hunting or roosting.

Date	Notes

LAPWING

Vanellus vanellus

Body length: *28-31cm*

Where to spot:

Coastal areas, marshes,

sea meadows

Resident

Our biggest plovers are often seen with other waders as they gather to look for worms on mudflats and coastal pasture in winter. They can form large flocks, and have a flappy flight with large rounded wings; their colouring is distinctive with the iridescent green-black plumage and long crest.

They nest on farmland and marshes so can struggle if not enought insects are available to feed their chicks.

An alternative name for the lapwing is peewit, after the bird's call, heard as they perfom their display flights.

Date	Notes

Haliaeetus albicilla

Body length: *76-92cm*

Where to spot:

Breeds in coastal regions

but flies long distances

Resident

WHITE-TAILED EAGLE

This eagle has recently been reintroduced to various parts of the country. It nests on cliffs or in tall trees nearby, and swipe fish from the water, though it can take birds and small mammals.

The white wedge-shaped tail of the adult is diagnostic, but the sheer size is what will be convincing; it really is huge with a wingspan of almost 2.5 metres.

It rarely calls apart from when it is near the nest, unlike the much smaller (but more familiar and similarly dark) buzzard that often makes its presence known vocally.

Date	Notes

AVOCET

Recurvirostra avosetta

Body length: *42-46cm*

Where to spot:

Open seashores, coastal

lagoons, sandy banks

Resident

The exquisite plumage and astonishing curved bill of this wader means it is recognisable more from its use as the RSPB logo than being commonly seen, as its breeding and wintering grounds are very localised in southern and eastern England.

They feed by sweeping that specialised bill back and forth, sifting invertebrates and crustaceans from the water and stirred mud.

The call is a piping "kwip-kwip-kwip" used to sound the alarm as well as for general communication.

Date	Notes

Saxicola torquata

Body length: *11-13cm*

Where to spot:

Dunes and scrubby areas

near the coast

Resident

STONECHAT

Chats are part of the thrush family (see wheatear) and this robin-sized bird often lives in coastal areas with gorse and tussocky grass where it both nests and hunts for its main food of insects.

The female has less dramatic markings: she lacks the black head and white collar of the male.

Stonechats have a good voice, with a sharp tack of alarm as well as a more melodious song with a slightly scratchy quality.

Date	Notes

DUNLIN

Calidris alpina

Body length: *17-21cm*

Where to spot:

Tidal flats, seaweedy

shorelines, estuaries

Winter visitor

Getting to know the size and colouring of a dunlin is a good idea, as many other waders are identified by their similarities or otherwise to this, our most widespread wader. Winter plumage is smooth and grey, and the slightly curved black bill and dark grey legs are a good starting point when faced with sorting out who's who in mixed flocks.

Dunlin prefer estuary mud and seaweedy shores to any other habitat, and are often seen in large numbers.

In the flock they will make a "pip-pip" call to each other.

Date	Notes

Arenaria interpres

Body length: *21-24cm*

Where to spot:

Pebbly shores, coastal

towns, harbours

Winter visitor

As the name suggests, turnstones work the pebbly margin at the strandline on a beach to find morsels buried under the seaweed, and often walk boldy and purposefully around piers and seafronts.

The dark ring above the white breast, and the wedge-shaped bill are good features to look for, along with the orange legs. Summer plumage is much more colourful but they have usually moved on before we see it in its full glory.

Rattly chuckles are made for both alarm and display.

Date	Notes

GANNET

Morus bassanus

Body length: *85-97cm*

Where to spot:

Rocky coastlines, steep cliffs, open seas

Resident

Gannets travel far across the ocean out of the breeding season, but when they do settle to nest, they choose steep cliffs and precipitous ledges on which to lay their eggs.

Adult gannets have an ochre head, blue bill edged in black, and black wing tips. The large black feet propel the bird through the water once it has performed its famous arrow-like stoop and dive to catch fish at depth.

Calls to each other at colonies consist of a loud raucous cackle. The sound from so many birds can be ear-splitting.

Date	Notes

Tringa totanus

Body length: *24-27cm*

Where to spot:

Coastal marshes and

pasture

Resident

REDSHANK

The red legs give this elegant wader its name, and it is the commonest medium-sized bird on mudflats and marshland. The fine black lines on the tail, broad white edges to the inside wing and red feet poking out make the redshank easy to spot when it flies off.

As with many waders, resident birds are joined by those migrating from more northerly areas, so can be seen on coasts as they pass through.

The redshank's calls are evocative and musical, with a mournful "tyoo-tyoo" and the "kyeep-kyeep" alarm call.

Date	Notes

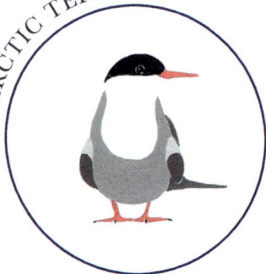

ARCTIC TERN

Sterna paradisaea

Body length: *33-39cm*

Where to spot:

Coasts, islands, harbours, steep cliffs

Summer visitor

These birds travel from the top of the planet to the bottom and back again on an annual basis, wintering in South Africa and Antarctica and breeding in colonies on our cliffs and coastlines during the summer.

The black cap, wholly red bill and short legs distinguish this tern from others, and terns are generally smaller and more finely-built than gulls. This streamlining is needed as they all make spectacular migrations.

The calls are varied, including a piping chatter and a hard rattle when arguing with the neighbours.

Date	Notes

More birds you may see:

CURLEW

KINGFISHER

BLACK REDSTART

KITTIWAKE

LINNET

*You will find
these in the
other books
in the series*

Notes & Sketches

Notes & Sketches

Index